Life in a Pride

Lions

Heinemann
LIBRARY

Richard and Louise Spilsbury

www.heinemann.co.uk/library

To order:
☎ Phone 44 (0) 1865 888066
🖹 Send a fax to 44 (0) 1865 314091
💻 Visit the Heinemann Bookshop at www.heinemann.co.uk/library to browse our catalogue and order online.

First published in Great Britain by Heinemann Library, Halley Court, Jordan Hill, Oxford OX2 8EJ, part of Harcourt Education.
Heinemann is a registered trademark of Harcourt Education Ltd.

Editorial: Nicole Irving and Georga Godwin
Design: Ron Kamen and Celia Floyd
Picture Research: Catherine Bevan and Charlotte Lippmann
Production: Lorraine Warner

Originated by Dot Gradations Ltd
Printed in China by Wing King Tong

ISBN 0 431 16923 3 (hardback)   ISBN 0 431 16930 6 (paperback)
07 06 05 04 03   08 07 06 05 04
10 9 8 7 6 5 4 3 2 1   10 9 8 7 6 5 4 3 2 1

British Library Cataloguing in Publication Data
Spilsbury, Richard and Spilsbury, Louise
Animal Groups: Lions – Life in a pride
599.7'57'156
A full catalogue record for this book is available from the British Library.

Acknowledgements

The publishers would like to thank the following for permission to reproduce photographs: Steve Bloom pp13, 23 (bottom); Bruce Coleman Collection p22; Corbis/Diego Lezama Orezzoli p27; FLPA/Minden Pictures pp23 (top), 25, /Philip Perry p21; Bational Geographic p20; Nature Picture Library/Anup Shah (BBC Wild) pp10, 18; NHPA/Andy Rouse pp7, 17, /Ann and Steve Toon p5, /Anthony Bannister pp11, 14, /J and A Scott p16, /John Shaw p8, /Martin Harvey p26, /Nigel J Dennis p9, /Daryl Balfour p28; Oxford Scientific Films/Hilary Pooley p4, /John Downer p15, /Rafi Ben-Shanar p24, /Stan Osolinski p19; Still Pictures p 6.

Cover photograph of an African lioness and cubs reproduced with permission of Bruce Coleman Collection/Erwin and Peggy Bauer.

The publishers would like to thank Claire Robinson for her assistance in the preparation of this book.

Every effort has been made to contact copyright holders of any material reproduced in this book. Any omissions will be rectified in subsequent printings if notice is given to the publishers.

Contents

Any words appearing in the text in bold, **like this**, are explained in the Glossary.

What are lions?

Lions are large, powerful cats with long bodies and tails. They are covered in short, thick fur that is mostly the same yellowish-brown colour all over. The only parts that are a different colour are their undersides (their tummies), which are often paler, and the back of their ears and tips of their tails, which are black. Lions are the only cats that have a tuft (fluffy end) to their tails.

Male and female

When fully grown, **male** lions are bigger than **female** lions, which are called lionesses. What makes them really easy to tell apart is the male's **mane**. This is a thick collar of longer fur that surrounds a male's face and neck. It makes the male look even bigger than he is. As a male gets older, his mane gets darker.

The lion is often called the 'king of the beasts' because it is so large and strong. Its mighty roar can be heard far and wide.

What are cats?

There are 37 different **species** (kinds) of wild cat in the world and most are similar to pet cats. They have round heads with large eyes, upright ears and long whiskers near their mouths. Many cats have patterned fur and soft padded paws. Tigers, leopards and cheetahs are other species of big cat. When people talk about big cats, they mean large wild cats.

Groups of lions

Most kinds of cat live, hunt and sleep alone. Lions are unusual cats because they live in groups. Even though you may see a lion alone, it is still part of a group and it returns to its group at some point. A group of lions is called a pride.

A fully grown lion can be around 1 metre tall and measure over 3 metres from nose to tail tip – about the same length as a small car!

What is a pride like?

A pride of lions usually includes around fifteen lions, but some may have as many as 40 members. Most of the lions in a pride are **females** and their young, along with two or three adult **males**.

The female lions in a pride are usually related. This is because lionesses tend to stay in the pride they are born in, while the young males move away when they are two or three years old. The pride is mostly made up of sisters, aunts, mothers and grandmothers who have all grown up together. One of the reasons lion prides work so well is that the females have been together for a long time, so they know and trust each other.

Although prides vary, a pride of lions often includes about two males, five lionesses, four young lions and three cubs (baby lions).

Alone and in groups

The whole pride is not together very often. Most of the time the male lions go around alone or with other males from the pride. The female lions spend their time in small groups with other females and their **cubs**. These groups may change every day, as lions spend time with different members of the pride.

Different roles in a pride

Male and female lions have different jobs in the pride. The females do most of the hunting. They get most of the food for themselves and the other lions in the pride. They also take care of the cubs. The males are the protectors of the pride. Their job is to defend the place the pride lives in against intruders.

A male lion's **mane** makes him look big and strong and helps him to scare off lions from other prides.

Where do prides of lions live?

Most prides of lions live in Africa. In the past, lions also lived throughout India, the Middle East and southern Asia. People have killed many of these lions or taken over their **habitats** for human use. Today, the only place you can find wild lions outside Africa is in one **national park** in India.

Lions live in habitats called **savannah** or **scrub**. These have a long, hot dry season, and a shorter season when heavy rain falls. There are a few trees and thorny bushes scattered about – sometimes even a little woodland – but it is too hot and dry for many large plants to grow. Lions prefer to live among big patches of dry grass, where there are good views of the animals they hunt.

The dry grasses of the savannah are the same yellowish-brown colour as most lions' fur. This **camouflage** helps lions to hide among the grasses while they are hunting.

How large is a pride's territory?

In places where there is lots of prey, a pride's territory is smaller than in an area where there are fewer animals to hunt. Some prides have territories that are over 250 square kilometres (96 square miles) in size (the area of a small city) to be sure of enough food for all the pride members.

A pride's patch

A pride of lions always lives in a particular area within their habitat, called their **territory**. They choose an area where plenty of **prey** animals live, such as gazelles, buffalo, zebra and antelope, so there is enough food for all the pride. Most territories also contain a **watering hole** – a lake or river where there is always water. In such a hot habitat, lions can die if they don't drink enough water.

Lions come to watering holes like this to drink and to catch other thirsty animals that visit.

Guarding the territory

Adult **male** lions spend a lot of their time guarding the pride's territory. They want to keep other lions out, because they might take the pride's food. The males walk around their territory in groups, like guards on patrol. If they find an intruder who has strayed into their territory, the males may try to kill it.

Scent marks

● ● ● ● ● ● ● ● ● ● ●

Male lions often spray strong-smelling urine (wee) onto trees, bushes, stones or paths inside their pride's territory. These are called **scent marks**. They tell other lions that the territory belongs to the pride. By sniffing, other lions can tell how long ago a pride male passed by on patrol – and can guess how safe it would be to stroll through the territory.

One way males mark their territory is by scuffing the ground with their claws. They scratch away at the ground with their back feet and sometimes urinate (wee) there, too.

What happens in a pride?

If you look around a pride's **territory** during the daytime, the chances are you won't see much. Lions spend most of their time asleep, resting or **grooming**. They usually lie out in the open, or under the shade of a tree, but are hard to spot because of their **camouflaged** fur. They become more active in the early evening. This is when the young **cubs suckle** (feed on milk) from their mothers and play. This is also when the adult lions hunt for food.

When groups of lionesses relax, they often stretch out with their heads, legs and tails draped over each other.

Grooming

Grooming is when animals lick and clean each other. Lionesses do most of the grooming in a pride. They groom each other as well as the cubs and males. Grooming keeps the lions clean and makes everyone feel like part of the pride.

Active lions

Adult lions may spend a lot of their active time walking around. They can walk for about 8 kilometres (5 miles) each day, searching for **prey**. When they do find prey, it takes a lot of strength to catch and kill it. That is why lions rest a lot during the day – to save their energy for hunting.

Feasting

Prides do not usually kill prey to eat every day. They are more likely to catch food every two or three days. After eating a really big meal, the pride may spend the next day or so just resting and letting their food go down. They don't need to hunt if their stomachs are full, but the extra weight also means they cannot run as fast.

What do lions eat?

Lions are **carnivores**, which means that they eat other animals. Lions prefer to eat large grazing animals (animals that eat grass), such as wildebeest (or gnu), zebra, antelope and buffalo. Sometimes they even hunt young giraffes and elephants. If they cannot catch big animals, they eat smaller ones, such as warthogs, hares and tortoises. If food is really scarce, lions will eat almost anything, including snakes, insects and even fruit.

The fact that a pride always lives in the same territory means that when the lions go hunting at night, they know where the best places are to find food.

13

How do lions catch their food?

Lions are good at catching animals for food. They have strong **muscles** in their chest and front legs for grabbing large **prey** and pulling it to the ground. A lion's paws have sharp, curved claws that can hook into a prey's skin, then its strong jaws clamp around the prey's throat.

Lions usually hunt at dawn or dusk, so they can sneak up on their prey. Lions have excellent **senses** of hearing and sight. They can hear prey almost 2 kilometres (1 mile) away and twist their ears to pinpoint where sound is coming from. Their golden eyes can see at night almost as well as human eyes can during the daytime!

A lion has 30 teeth. It uses its four pointed **canine** teeth to hold the prey, kill it and tear the meat. Its other teeth bite through tough skin. Lions don't have teeth for chewing, because they swallow chunks of meat whole.

If the prey glances up while a lion is hunting, the lion freezes (suddenly stands still) to avoid being spotted.

Stalking and jumping

Lions are too heavy to run quickly for long. Most of their prey animals can run faster than they can. This is why lions have to **stalk** (sneak up on) their prey. At first, they move slowly and quietly towards the prey, crouching close to the ground and hiding behind plants. They watch the prey carefully all the time and when they are close enough, rush out and jump on it.

Takeaways

To avoid the hard work of hunting, lions often **scavenge** – steal food killed by other animals. Lions notice the tell-tale signs of vultures circling in the sky, or hyenas calling. These animals are good at finding **carrion** (dead animals), so lions can follow them to a free meal!

Do lions hunt together?

The lionesses usually hunt the food for a pride. By hunting together they can catch more **prey**. They can also combine their strength to pull down much bigger animals than they could alone.

Lionesses often divide into smaller groups when hunting. Different lionesses have different jobs in the hunt. Larger, heavier lionesses wait to catch running prey. Faster, lighter lionesses chase it towards them.

When they attack a herd of prey animals, lionesses often go for the younger or weaker members because they run more slowly.

Hunting tactics

Sometimes lionesses form a line and chase prey into a dead end, such as a **watering hole**. The animals panic and try to run back the way they came, straight into the waiting lions. At other times, lionesses form a wide circle around a herd (group) of prey and close in on it.

Lazy males?

Male lions usually trail behind the lionesses when they hunt. They don't take part in chasing and catching prey, but as soon as an animal is caught, they run up and demand to eat first and to eat the most – the lion's share. A male lion can eat 34 kilograms of meat in one meal.

Mealtime squabbles

When the hunters have caught an animal, the other lions in the pride run up. Male lions eat first, but the **females** complain angrily until they get a turn. **Cubs** have to wait until last. It is quite common for lion cubs to starve to death in their first year because they cannot get enough food.

At mealtimes, lions growl, snarl and snap at each other. If the other lions did not make such a fuss, the males might go on eating until there was nothing left.

Does the pride care for the cubs?

When a lioness becomes an adult, she can **mate** with the older **males** in the pride. Her **cubs** (baby lions) are born about fourteen weeks later. Lionesses usually have three or four cubs at a time. At first, the cubs are small and helpless. They are blind for two weeks and cannot run for a month, so the mothers have to take good care of them.

Lions' lairs

Lions do not make homes that they live in all the time, but when they have cubs, lionesses keep them in **lairs**. A lair is any place where the cubs can be well hidden from hyenas, leopards and other **predators**. It could be a space between some bushes or fallen trees, or a dip in the ground.

Mothers move their cubs from one lair to another, to keep them safe. They carry the cubs gently by the neck.

18

Growing up in a pride

One of the reasons lions live in a pride is so the cubs are well cared for. A mother lion may leave her cubs for whole days and nights, while she hunts or relaxes with other lions from the pride. The cubs survive because they can **suckle** from any of the lionesses with cubs in their pride. These other lionesses also act as babysitters, looking after the cubs while their mother is away.

Watch and learn

Young cubs in a pride learn a lot from watching what the older lions do. They also learn as they play, because they are practising skills they will need when they are older. For example, when a mother lion flicks her tail for her cub to chase, the cub is learning how to pounce on fast-moving **prey**.

Young cubs practise fighting with other cubs as there is no risk of being badly hurt.

19

How do lions communicate?

When we want to tell someone something, we can **communicate** it in different ways. As well as talking, we send messages using our face and body, for example by frowning or smiling, pointing or waving. Lions have different ways of communicating, too. They tell other lions how they feel or pass on information using sounds, movements, scents or touch.

Sounds lions make

Lions make at least nine different sounds, including growls, snarls and miaows. Different sounds mean different things. The most familiar lion sound is the roar, which can be heard up to 9 kilometres (6 miles) away. Lions usually roar in the evening or after feeding. The roar reminds lions who don't belong to the pride who the **territory** belongs to. It warns them to keep out!

Roaring together tells lions from other prides to keep away, and it also makes the lions in the pride feel more like a team.

Soft and loud

Lions can make each of their sounds louder or softer depending on what they want to communicate. When mothers call their **cubs**, they make low, quiet grunting sounds. Cubs miaow to greet their mothers and purr when they are content. The lionesses use slightly louder grunts to keep in contact with each other when they are out hunting, especially when it is dark.

Body language

If they are close enough to each other, lions use body language – movements and positions – to communicate the way they feel. A flicking tail and head kept low mean the lion is threatening to attack. When their mouths are open without showing their teeth, young lions want to play. Lions bare their teeth to show they are angry or ready to attack.

A lion's black lips, ear backs and tail tuft make any movements of these parts more obvious. This lioness's partly open mouth, erect tail and pricked ears signal to others that she has spotted possible **prey**.

21

Keeping the pride together

Most of the time, the lions in a pride get along well. They constantly show each other affection by sitting or lying close together, rubbing against each other, **grooming** and licking one another's faces, especially after feeding. Doing these things helps to keep the members of the pride together and reminds them they are all part of a team or family.

The greeting ceremony

When members of a pride meet, they always greet each other in the same way. First they sniff each other's noses, then they moan softly, rub heads, then sides and drape their tails across each other's backs. It's rather like the way we kiss or hug our families to say we are pleased to see them.

The greeting ceremony is an important way for lions to prove to each other that they belong to the same pride.

Lions use smell as a way of identifying pride members. Because they are always grooming, rubbing heads and licking each other, the lions in a pride share a similar smell.

Lions from the same pride sometimes fight, especially over food. To stop the fight the weaker of the two lions may lie on its back. This says to the stronger lion 'I give up', and the fight stops.

23

Do prides change?

A pride stays together for a long time, but every few years there is a change. **Female** members of a pride stay together for many years, but all young **males** leave their prides when they are two or three years old.

Why do males leave?

The older males – the father lions – often chase the young males out of the pride. These males form a gang. They roam about together for several years until they are old and strong enough to try to take over a pride of their own. To do this they have to challenge the adult male lions of that pride to a fight. If they win, they will take over the pride and its **territory**.

When they first leave their mother's pride, a gang of young males hunt in other prides' territories while keeping out of the way of the owners.

After a male leader of a pride is beaten in a fight, he is often badly wounded and may die. Sometimes he escapes, but he will not be able to return to the pride.

Running a pride

Males usually control a pride when they are at their strongest and fittest, around five or six years old. Most adult males only get to control a pride for about two or three years. After this, they are weaker, so when younger males try to take over their pride, they lose the fight.

Cub killing

When new male lions take over a pride, they usually kill all the cubs they find there. This seems cruel to us, but they do this so that the females are ready to mate with them sooner. Usually, lionesses can only have new cubs when their other cubs are nearly two. If they lose cubs, they can mate a few days later. This means the new leaders become the fathers of all the cubs in the pride. This is why all the cubs in a pride are about the same age.

What dangers threaten a pride?

Living in a pride protects lions from many dangers. The fact that lions usually stay in a group means that they have hardly any **predators** (animals that try to kill them). If a lion is injured, it can still feed on meat the others have caught, until it is well again. If a lioness is killed, other lionesses in the pride look after her **cubs**.

Lions at risk

Cubs are most at risk. Leopards, hyenas and even **male** lions from other prides try to catch and eat young cubs. Adult lions can be hurt when catching **prey**. Some are injured or killed by zebra, giraffe or buffalo kicks, or the bites of snakes and crocodiles. That is why lions must kill their prey quickly, before they get hurt.

Hyenas work in teams, and can kill an adult lion if it is injured. If food is scarce, hyenas may even fight with a healthy lion for **carrion**.

Are lions man-eaters?

Lions do sometimes attack people, but it is unusual. An old lion with worn teeth or one that has been wounded may turn into a man eater, because humans are easier to catch than faster prey. But most of the time, lions try to avoid people because people have weapons that can kill them.

Because lions live in open areas, hunters and herders can hunt them easily.

People – a pride's greatest threat

The greatest threat to any pride is humans. Farmers or **herders** kill many lions each year. They do this because lions can kill and eat farm animals, such as cattle, that belong to them. Some countries still allow hunters to shoot lions for sport. This can greatly damage a pride, because hunters usually try to kill the biggest males. If they kill a leader male from a pride, the pride will then be taken over by a new male, who will kill all the cubs.

Nowhere to live, nothing to eat

The other way humans are a danger to lions is by destroying the **habitats** lions live in. In Africa, people are taking over more and more land to build farms and towns. When there are fewer areas of grass for **grazers** like zebras to feed on, they die. Grazing animals are a lion's main food, so prides of lions gradually starve and die because there are fewer animals for them to eat.

Protecting prides

Many African countries are working hard to protect lions. They set up areas where no one is allowed to take land for building or farming, or harm the animals. These protected areas are called **national parks** or **reserves**, and in them prides of lions can get on with their lives in peace.

This pride of lions lives in the safety of the Chobe National Park in Africa.

Lion facts

Where do lions live?

This map shows where most of the lions in the world live today. There are also around 300 Asian lions in the Gir Forest **National Park** in Gujarat, Western India.

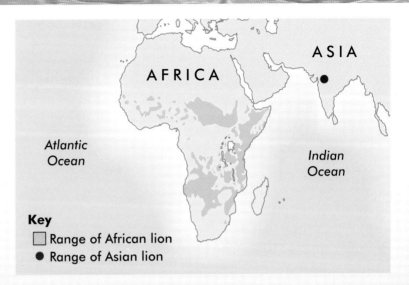

ASIA

AFRICA

Atlantic Ocean

Indian Ocean

Key
- ☐ Range of African lion
- ● Range of Asian lion

Vital statistics

Lions live up to fifteen to twenty years.

Top speed

Lions usually walk slowly. When they hunt, they can run as fast as a car (up to 60 kilometres (37 miles) per hour) but only for a short distance. Lions are not great climbers, but they lie on large, low branches.

Amazing vision

Lions can see well in the dark because they have a special layer in their eyes. If even a tiny amount of light gets into their eyes, this layer reflects it around inside their eyes so they can see.

Lion cubs

When lion **cubs** are born they weigh about 1.4 kilograms. Their fur is spotted at first as **camouflage** (to help them hide from **predators**). They drink milk from the mothers in the pride until they are about seven months old. Then they are ready to feed on meat with the other lions. They join in hunts from about eleven months old.

Glossary

camouflage   colours and patterns that help an animal's body blend in with its background

canine   long pointed teeth at the front of an animal's mouth

carnivores   animals that mostly eat other animals

carrion   meat eaten from an animal that is found dead

communicate   pass on information to another person or animal

cubs   baby lions

female   animal that, when mature, can become a mother. A female human is called a woman or a girl.

grazer   animal that eats grass or other plants. Grazers, such as zebra, usually live in herds (large groups).

grooming   when animals lick or clean each other

habitat   place where an animal or plant lives. There are many different habitats around the world, including forests and deserts.

herders   people who take herds of animals into the countryside for them to graze (feed on plants)

lair   place where lion cubs can be well-hidden, such as a space between some bushes or fallen trees

male   animal that, when mature, can become a father. A male human is called a man or a boy.

mane   collar of fur around an adult male lion's neck. A mane makes a lion look bigger and stronger and protects the lion's neck when he fights.

mate   after a male and female lion have mated, a lion cub (baby) begins to grow inside the female

muscles   parts of the body that help to make the bones in the body move

national park   area that is protected by law, so that people cannot harm the plants and animals that live there

predators   animals that hunt or catch other animals to eat them

prey   animals that are hunted or caught by other animals for food

reserves   areas of protected land where animals can live safely

savannah   large, open area of land mostly covered in grasses, but with patches of woodland

scavenge   steal food from other animals

scent marks   when an animal sprays strong smelling urine (wee) somewhere as a signal to other animals

scrub   areas with sandy soil that have patches of trees and shrubs

senses   animals have some or all of the following senses: hearing, sight, touch, smell and taste

species   group of living things that are similar in many ways and can reproduce together

stalk   quietly sneak up on prey in order to get close enough to catch it

suckle   when a baby animal drinks its mother's milk

territory   area within a habitat that an animal claims as its own

watering hole   place where animals go often to drink water

30

Find out more

Books

In the Wild: Lions, Claire Robinson (Heinemann Library, 1999)
Eyewitness Guides: Cat, Juliet Clutton-Brock (Dorling Kindersley, 2000)
Life Cycles: Cats and other Mammals, Sally Morgan (Belitha Press, 2000)
Natural World: Lion, Bill Jordan (Hodder Wayland, 1999)
Nature Fact Files: Big Cats, Rhonda Klenvansky (Southwater Publications, 2000)
Our Wild World: Lions, Cherie Winner (North Word Publications, 2002)

Websites

www.bbc.co.uk/reallywild/amazing/lion.shtml
www.nationalgeographic.com/kids/creature_feature/lions
www.worldalmanacforkids.com
www.bornfree.org.uk
http://wildnetafrica.co.za/envirokids/ourbig5/lifeasalion.html

Index